KERRI CULL

soak

1 Stamp's Lane, St. John's, NL, Canada, A1E 3C9
WWW.BREAKWATERBOOKS.COM

ISBN 978-1-55081-380-7
Copyright © 2012 Kerri Cull
A CIP catalogue record for this book is available
from Library and Archives Canada.

We acknowledge the support of the Canada Council for the
Arts which last year invested $24.3 million in writing and
publishing throughout Canada. We acknowledge the Government
of Canada through the Canada Book Fund and the Government of
Newfoundland and Labrador through the Department of Tourism,
Culture and Recreation for our publishing activities.

PRINTED AND BOUND IN CANADA.

Canada Council for the Arts	Conseil des Arts du Canada

Breakwater Books is committed to choosing papers
and materials for our books that help to protect our
environment. To this end, this book is printed on a recycled
paper that is certified by the Forest Stewardship Council®.

MIX
Paper from
responsible sources
FSC® C011825

FOR MY PARENTS, MARGARET AND CARL CULL

stretch

NIGHT GAMES

3-2-1 you're it
They yell, sound formed by Chiclet smiles.
Slight fingernails are founded by dirt,
food, sand and polish.

Red rover red rover
They call me over and they receive
my jumbo fingers scrubbed clean
and bloodless.

Miss Mary Mack Mack Mack
Younger girls clap near the swing set;
older ones stand behind the gate,
breasts struggling to escape baby tees.

10-9-8
Spotlights swerve across the slow night.
I flick the switch of my desk lamp and
the sun
throws bakeapples across the sky.

Ready or not here I come

I SPY

I kissed you
over and over
lying in a field
behind my house.
Quick
kid kisses
on your chapped
five-year-old lips:
one
one-two
one-two-three
one-two-three-four
one-two-three-four-five
counting touches
in a pretend bed, until
Mom called me
for dinner.

I jumped up
scared,
thinking
she saw us,
kissing
in the grass,
glowing
with girl pink
shame.

We stood there in your bathroom—
breasts stretching against training bras
hips restless under baby fat
looking at each other—
pants pulled down to knees

still scratched from bike falls and cement picnics.
You had more hair than me.
I can still see the very white flesh under peppered strands
circling down to places then unknown.

SECOND-HAND

Her itty-bitty six-year-old body bends
over an experienced suitcase.
She pulls at the inner elastic.
Her brother, wearing those old-fashioned
upside-down glasses he found
at the fifty-year-old flea market,
is holding it up so it doesn't collapse
on her bony-bare legs.

There are mismatched shoes everywhere.
Suits hang on wrought-iron fences,
smells of aftershave and fir trees rise among
dolls, toys, purses strewn across boxes.
Children rummage through ragged baggage
clutching coins,
putting noses to leather,
wool, cotton.

Between scattered stories and stained books
he finds a party hat and
an old Willie the Wise-Guy comic.
He turns to his sister.
Paintings are poised against boxes
or collapsing from the push of people.
She sits securely on the edge of a curb
next to an old, faded, wood-framed Jesus.

SUPERHEROES

Two little girls squish grey footprints into fresh cement.
Their hands reach forward, delicate as cats' claws,
grabbing at people that graze their coats,
trying to evolve into this new decade as different beings.

The sidewalk narrows and disappears
into concrete distance: two girls'
steps quicken; they exhale, silently, their invisible
power over everything that passes.

A TURNIP

       lying on its side
against the ice-covered curb,
down
in the dip of Carpasian Road.

Its cantaloupe flesh dirty and dry,
disguised by spider webs of ice.
It asked itself why its vitals were freezing,
why it was not on a dinner plate, warm and
awaiting its trip down tubes
into red-walled oblivion.

No, it was cold and waiting—
for hypothermia, for death;
lying there
cast off
against a curb, sorrowful. So
I picked it up, I
brought it home.

NOVA

When I was no more worn than
a freshly hemmed pair of pants,
my dreams were big. I wanted to be

like Joni Mitchell, bojangle myself
to the big yellow taxi
in the big blue clouds

or like the people I saw
through my closed
nighttime vinyl blinds.

I would sit on my bed
body folded looking out through
shoulders, hips, lips and wood.

Words and worlds had no boundaries.
I was just a girl in a gigantic world
made up of star stuff.

GOLDFISH

Accessory to murder at a very young age.
My victim: a goldfish.

Dad and I hovered over the toilet
and I swear I saw that fish swimming for its life
against the man-made current
as it was swept down to who knows where.

I stood, dripping tears, peering
into the toilet,
Dad's hand on my shoulder,
and then turned to pack for summer vacation
thankful I didn't have to worry if the goldfish
would survive three weeks without us.

CANDY

Ten years old and two dollars in my pocket.
Ginger ale and marshmallow strawberries,
fries with dressing and gravy,
and shelves of convenient foods.

The days I went home with
jellies, gummies, anything but chocolate,
Dad would shake his head:
Tsk tsk tsk.
If anything will kill you, that will.

This from a man who ice fishes
at the beginning of winter,
boats without a life jacket,
and never did learn how to swim.

PUSHED OVER

Ice shadows licked the sunshine's
iridescent sweat.

A father and son
idly stood
in the park.

Parents pulled kids up on greasy toboggans.
Family dogs chased jellybean snowsuits
down fondant hills.

Four days later my boys were exactly the same—
happy and bloated, bulbous
bodies stuffed from too many holiday goodies—but

they were in three parts,
pushed over,
decapitated.

The twig nose, the rock eyes,
the same crooked mouths
were still smiling.

FIGHT CLUB

I thought the swan was going to eat him—
rip him to bits, leave me there, alone, to die.
The swan was a dainty dinosaur;
my dad, the world's strongest man.

Unthankful for our bread-crumb sacrifice,
that water-hose neck came to a point at the beak,
hatched a sound of hate.

Mouth agape and wings unfurling,
it chased my dad down the side of the bank,
while I stood there with sugar-cube tears.

I had visions of clawing and slashing, of pigeons and ducks
rallying around fight-club style, my dad nowhere to be found,
and shreds of my lemony shirt left on the swampy ground.

I'm still afraid of big giant-necked birds on walking trails,
still bring bread, sunflower seeds, lettuce
to satiate their hunger, their hate,
their instinct.

SWEET

Purple shirts and big glasses,
blond sweaters, white pearls
smiling.

Fierce—
you locked yourself away
and swallowed hard candy.

You had forgotten
the man who made you
and the woman who named you.

For years we danced
and sang during sleep.
We were perfect,
sticky and sweet:

jewels among minutiae
waiting to grow.

MAKE-UP

Braille dots of mascara line her eyelids,
a hint of hazard for those
paying attention.

Hair, a question-mark ponytail,
except for one piece curved to the slope of her head,
crossing her forehead and secure behind her ear.

Jeans rest on her bursting flesh, keeping her together.
She used to look like a doll, wore glasses at three:
big innocent eyes with no idea what they would see.

They say it happens to half of us
but did they include you in that percentage?
Brother, cat, dog, thirteen years
and all the rest of it?

PLAYING

she'd played hockey
with these three
since she was wee

when they were seventeen
they asked her to a party
and right there them three

unravelled her faith

the next week
the other kids called her
slut.

BREAKING BREAD

She ruined food for the rest of his life.
Sitting at lunch eating spam and cheese, teasing
his brother but saying it was he
who didn't belong.

He would eat in his bedroom from then on
as meals continued in the next room.
How could they know that he would never
want to share a table with anyone again

or that he'd be hard to live with
and angry and envious of perfect families?
How could they know they'd changed
the shape of him?

WHAT I REALLY WANTED
TO BE WAS A CAT

I curve my form
to catch the sun.
Plop down in a perfect circle
of conviction and calm.
My sinewy neck twists

to lick my thigh.
My velcro tongue
protrudes with instinct.

Blinds of light filter through the room
as I curl my coin-size paws
into a fist.
I lap and gnaw and look around
with squinted, saffron eyes.

Then my paw bursts open—a flower
blossoming in fast forward
as if I am learning to count to five,
clean my face for the first time,
wave.

run

BEDLAM

Destination
Fort Nelson
British Columbia
Left home
following a dream on my own volition
across Canada in seven days
three friends
dope and a thousand dollars
it wasn't big and shiny and silver
girlfriend
iguana
cat
hedgehog
plumber's assistant
house painter
mill worker
the new year
trying to stay out of
bedlam
graveyard shift for four years
bat's eye to the night
shingles
diarrhea
stomach flu
hemorrhoids
two weeks sick leave
not a day more
my life in a cube van
pantyhose holding it tight
it was seven years
say thank you
leave again
before it gets a grip

HOLES IN YOUR JEANS

Holes in your jeans:
breathing places for things unsaid.
You tried to write over your self
with bandanas and sheets of canvas
drenched in memories
you wished would leave.

Songs of broken vows,

long-lost tastes of once-loved music
were disguised by grown-ups
you thought you knew.

It was sad days,
coming and ending
until every second
of ten years had passed.
And you lived through it—

shouting dissonance.

BRUISED

These whitewashed walls were bruised
in places where pictures used to hang.
That first night we unpacked
everything backwards:
bed, sofa, no sheets or pillows.
We used ourselves and nothing but the still stench air
of the last livyer to warm us.
I draped a fisherman's sweater across my legs.

Months later and we have everything here.

The towels have their own place in the narrow
linen closet.
The glasses, plates and bowls have their own homes
next door to their smaller partners.
Everything is in its picture-perfect place.
There's a new smell

But the air is the same—
unfamiliar—
like that first night
we slept in our sweaters.

TOES LIKE GRAPES

We lie on the couch: a puzzle completed—
feet to face, your soles stare at me and
I can't help but put my palms to them.

Your baby toe is small, very small
just sitting above the wide width
of your flat feet.

The pads on your toes like grapes:
full, tender,
soft to squeeze.

Skin thickens on the side
of your biggest toe. I touch it and
blood blushes again.

You can barely feel it, just see me
removing and undoing leftover dirt
and fast walking from your day.

Each line in your foot curving, smiling at me
like laugh lines. I press them with my thumbs
and my palms cup them like the curve of a face.

THE FAT CAT

at grafenbergs
I watch your features light

the mark belbin band
saxophone bass drum
guitar no vocals

harmonies stick to air
hanging smoke thick

metronome on my neck
gently pulsing sound like blood

candles flicker stars

we shift to the door
make way down snow-covered steps
to listen to blues

fat cat door is closed
smoke hugging us from the cold
pulling us inside

swathed in dark dusk
we listen to the music

your hand on my thigh
rubbing notes on me

WHO OWNS THE
ABANDONED SHOES

flung over wires
like public lynchings,
an arrow
to a local crack house,
or marker of some adolescent folklore?

A single running shoe
lies on its side
in the middle
of the highway.

A pair of polished
men's leather shoes sleep
in the middle
of a busy bar-filled street.

Soles so dirty sometimes
you can hear their travel stories.
Other times so clean,
unworn,

hanging in the air
like an inflection—
unsure and
inexperienced.

TURTLE

A turtle is not a puppy.
A turtle in a big cardboard box with
P U P P Y marked in big bubble letters
is still not a puppy:
swampy leather purse,
a yarmulke.

You hated him.

Three years later
Hammy was the size of a tub of margarine
and deli meat was his food of choice.
He had all the world to explore
but was so g o d d a m n slow,
so generally bored
with life.

When you were 25, you left him
with your parents.
He escaped
one night. He
was coming to find you.

Winter passed,
glacial and sharp
and there he was, living in the backyard,
a universe to his little feet
filled with worms and moisture and earth.

That fall
your dad built him
a hibernation swamp—a turtle paradise—
and in went Hammy for the very last time.

He's still there, at your parents' house,
sitting on a side table,
shellacked,
mouth agape,
tongue
protruding.

ZIPLINE

Ok, the harness can hold 1,500 lbs and the zipline can hold
16,000 lbs. Just breathe. A car plus me inside. That just doesn't
sound right. Breathe. Check all requirements for that one
malfunction that pushes me out of the line. No luck. Smile.
You don't need to show emotion in public. Just do it. Breathe.
Ahem. Amen. It's my turn.

Hooked in.
Double check everything. Twice.
Two steps forward. Back again. Twice.

Slowly
walk,

       walk

           off

               the

                    platform

                        and the zip

                              dips

and then straightens out again.

My jaw clenches shut my hands grip the line thinking that's the
only reason I'm above ground you don't even have to hold on I
scream I think screaming is lame the falls rush below me as if
gathering speed to whisk my body down the mountain the
trees are offended by me I am disrupting their calm I land on
my back in the most graceful and delicate way possible my fear
abusing life around me but I did it and the line supported me
this one and only time.

And the mountain looked on
laughing at our arrogant assumption
that we had fooled it into submission.

ISLAND

Driving across this island
is like a full day's work
with a half-hour lunch break.

The scene changes as the sky
and we move west
from the isthmus
to Humber Valley.

We count fast hours:
only five and a half to
South Brook, where we
stay for the night to visit your parents;

coffee stops in Clarenville and Grand Falls;
bathroom breaks in Gander and Deer Lake.
The only ones with us
are the streams of trees—

from fir to frosted birch.
Each town like a shift over with:
two hours to Gander, then
one to Corner Brook.

We don't do anything
that leaves the other alone
on the road.
We talk and listen
and
there's hardly enough time

for quiet during sips and
breaths between laughter,
moose behind trees,
forests behind words.

OVERLOOKING THEIR KITCHEN

Twenty-two 26'ers of Newfie Screech
lined across two mature mahogany ledges where once
stood sport trophies, candles or some inordinate spoon collection,

like scrapbooks, family albums:
each bottle from a different night with a different assortment of people,
each story unlike the next. They are statements—

maybe a boast about the perfect taste of a drunk-strong liquor,
a weak, collapsing kidney or a toast to all the shots
swallowed and parties endured.

They drink this liquor along with India, Dominion, or
Quidi Vidi; there are no cosmopolitans or olives
calling from the edge of a decorative drinking counter.

The bottles make sure of this, standing there at attention
overlooking the kitchen where every Sunday night a poker game
takes place. They hope the winner is an inhabitant of the house

so they can keep all small dainty rainbow drinks with accessories
like umbrellas or cherries away from the ledge. They want the night
to last long after the last hand of the night has been played

and for another soldier to strengthen their army,
weaken someone's insides or maybe just keep
the thumb and finger drinks away.

ISOLATION

I am the woman in this poem

alone on this page wishing
for a coffee stain or a cigarette burn
or a crumb

waiting silently for you to study
my curves and edges like a loved
one

hoping you'll hover
on my words
mark my margins
care enough to question me
with an argument

WISH

you wanted a grow-old-together marriage

where time sits on experiences,
memories
thick and strong against
bruises and bleeding

punctuated by pet deaths
and vacation plans gone wrong
measured by wrinkles and
a shared headstone
your progeny placing gerbera daisies
and red roses on your resting place

SPICE

I rang in that new year with spices.

Cayenne pepper blazed
with heat like the last time
you made spaghetti and
I licked the wooden spoon.

Ground ginger, salmon
and maple syrup.
April. Tired skies,
red onion and sticky pink fingers.

Homegrown oregano,
olive oil and slick lips
sliding over each other
above a tabletop once set for two.

OPENING

The newly single woman sits next to her
plush orange sofa pillows
flipping magazine pages
as if asking questions.
She presses the spongy tip
of her gloss applicator to
her perfectly posed mouth.

This newly single woman makes chicken parm for two
and saves half for tomorrow's lunch.
She sits with the TV on in the background
and enjoys the taste of food folding
over her tongue.

The single woman goes shopping for no reason
but to find that perfect kitchen mat and returns it
the next day when she finds it's half an inch too short.
She has her fridge stocked with walnuts,
peaches, turnovers and plums.
She has the perfect reading lamp next to her bed
and glasses lie sleepily over the open book.

The single woman drinks tea after supper
and watches the news,
calls her sister to have a chat,
makes her own space
and sits in it
honestly.

APARTMENT

You always slept on our unforgiving couch.
It was faded to a feverish sand on the arms
and where bottoms sat the most.
The pillow and blanket fought for your comfort
against springs prodding your back.
You slept there for hours that year
in sequences of two or three.

Little pieces of you fell between the folds.
Leftover alcohol on your breath,
garlic, cigarette smoke—
it all clung to the walls.
Sinking into the wood of us that
was covered again by new flavours
of food and stains of our breath and build.

Our skin is all over that apartment—
ledge corners, tops of door frames, book spines—
remaining silently the same.

READING

on-tap
bar morphs
Edvard Munch
everyone's eyes
same direction
words cover
cozy silence
bartender and reader
power increases with every passing word
mouth phrases: *do you need anything?*
or are you all right?

covered by a blanket
words unevenly positioned
change on the bar stops rattling
movements become
threatening and enlarged
rum when replaced
clinks loudly
pop dispenser shushes fountain spray
clock ticks a countdown
clapping and talking arouse
rising sounds
quarters fall
the quiet draws our senses to attention
and then as if on cue
unleashes sound

AFTER THAT ARGUMENT

I fell asleep and
had a dream:

A paper lion was within me,
thin onion skinned
and translucent in fluorescent light.

I could limn its outline
above my tracing paper skin, picture
its furry sides standing up with static.

It marked its territory inside me with a paw print—
large, flowery, and deep.
It was strong and patient, waiting

to butterfly kiss you
with its eyelashes, to cover
you in papercuts.

LAVA

I went to the 53rd parallel to explore the rarities of my life
with porcupines, wolves and
snow at the end of August.

Our new house left us old markers of a little girl's home:
a pink Barbie shoe, a magenta pencil,
a class picture under the fridge.

Everyone said the first winter would be the worst.
We'd have to embrace the blankness of white.
Open our mouths to our cold cupcake world.

And after ten years of skyline montages
Winter's fury brought us to life and
we found a man and a woman still in love.

So we painted the dining room lava
and lived in our own quiet rebellion,
pouring sweat into our whitewashed world.

bend

MARK

Our fingerprints float in wine
lingering
between curves of
an oversized glass.

I drink them up
between the folds of my hands
an extension of us
ripe with age.

When I take the last sip
heat will resonate within me.
Your mark will slide over my insides
and I will blush red.

CEMETERY

I saw a burial—
the semicircle of mourners—
from fields away.

Headstones read deaths
back two hundred years.
Chipped granite gravestones
saluted ground before
meeting crosses.

In the night they stood like
wizened girls in white dresses
dancing slowly and swaying.

But when you'd look, they'd stop,
and stand firm.

PASSING

Back when cars had hips
you'd go to the lookout
and sit together
gazing out over an ocean
not knowing that
decades later
you'd be looking across
the same expanse,
grandchildren in tow,
wondering
where the time went.

SWELL

There are landscapes and
tracks in your hands,
thin and seasoned with brown sugar.

Pearly strands fall
over your face where
sponge and eyelids
swell.

You pull back
and look away,
hide your eyes
from a smaller pattern of you.

UNDERNEATH

Your lavender blouse
bunches under your arm,
breasts low and oppressed
from fifteen births and
a body pruned for work.

Wrinkles crawl connecting roots
breaking ground.

You reach for a candy and your
wide-knuckled hand shows
what it takes to make
the land move
and to keep it still.

FRAGMENT

When he first slug-walks into the bar his beer is waiting for him
from an icebox that holds nine Blue Star.
He shakes when pouring the first but after the next five
he's smoother than the tap itself.

He's four hundred pounds, his neck a rooster's sag
growing with bumps and scabs.
His chair disappears under the folding fat curves
a boiled, thick, overflowing soup.

He used to eat spoonfuls of butter
before he and his friends went beer-drinking,
said it would help ward off the grease-hunger
bound to come the next day.

His wife of forty years died two years ago, lung cancer
he tells me, getting up to leave,
his jacket trying to stretch across his bear-broad back.
I check the seat for urine as he walks out the door.

My eyes fix on the back of his neck
piglike in its bruised pinkness.
I smell him there like a familiar mattress
wondering if he'll be back same time next day.

MILES

Ice cream was your favourite thing.
Blue veins prove life.
Movement brings blood to slack
elbows and long, weighted earlobes.
You have memories of a younger you.

You are heavy with the past and
two mute women staring into the air,
visitors coming and going like waiters
scripted and hurried.
Someone got into your fruit basket last night.
That was us. Remember?
You ate the grapes and I ate the banana.

You looked at me trying to spark memory,
peeling back time, trying to find a name for my face.
You still have good eyes and ears like a cat
but your legs have given out—that's why you're here.

Now you're just waiting for a spot.
You're not sick. Just waiting for a stranger
to see you to your deathbed.

I should have brought you ice cream.

LINGERING

my mother was the mistress of her kitchen
her small body would sweat the stove's heat
smile widening with the thickening of the gravy

the birch tree outside flicks the window
branches covered with pale green leaves
click like a clock against glass

the tree sends a slight breeze into the air, smells
of onion and oregano stick to the walls
of the kitchen and her skin

shadowed by her silhouette this room becomes
a lingering impression of her body imprinted
like the smell of old flower beds

HOUSES

are born by labour pains of the earth
and the conviction
       to push themselves
            into existence. They
wake at night
colicky and bored, swaying
and whistling nighttime lullabies,
stirring in the morning, humming
and yawning in light.

They impose their conforming
right angles and rectangular doors,
and become the most trustworthy best friends
holding secrets tightly like the nails
that keep them together.

They change as they age,
start to shrink and sink and settle
like headstones;
grow sleepy
with years·
and the weight of others,
preserve the safe smells of the familiar.

I dance in mine, in the buttery light
of dusk, caramel sweet,
slow
and long,
like
forgiveness.

SKATING

I could not
understand why
when he lay dying
my father would watch
figure skating
over
and over
again.
　　　　Then
he told me
his childhood
was spent outside,
skating

on fragile
frozen ponds.

SCHIZOPHRENIA

The ground is rising
toward this hospital window once again.
Made it to half-way dead
this time.
Hand once held a knife
aimed at my mom.
She doesn't get along
even though they are in the next room.
Cousin's mouth argued
with my fingers.
She ran from my room. I thought she liked
my paintings.
Gave her one of a lone man swimming in a
deserted lake.
Lit a match over my paint-thinner body
to finish the rest.
Spent six weeks as a monster and
it finally worked.

UPSTREAM

Leaving the pub
your eyes settled on youth
that hurdled past with all the brightness
and sadness for which you had once firmly lived.

Years later in the water of the Humber River
you swam with salmon travelling
against time into crowded obscurity.

Tiny determined bodies twitching and pulsing
bursting with colour and mercury,
they reminded you of the day
you walked out of darkness

surrounded by sparkling lovers
twisting with the current.

FEDORA

You were hard to live with she said.
Beef iron wine, moonshine and whisky
and your wiry five-foot body dancing
on a plate if you were really feeling it.

You sat hat slanted
in your wicker rocking chair and lived
for eight more years.

You left me that tweed fedora
with thin traces of thick smells and colourless hair
now protected by plastic—
a bookmark in my life,
a monument.

WAITING

I am

And your bruised jaundiced eyelids
with cells full of nothing
are still bleeding.

And you're walking into my dream
all of us
sitting at the table
waiting.

And you say to us
I wasn't really dead.
I just fell asleep.
I was swimming.
I was.

THE BIGHT

Water holds memories here
little pockets and bubbles a few feet from shore

Childhoods shaped by capelin
drying on a flake

Shanty wharfs
crack to pinfish and pebbles

Footprints of old children
settled in graves

Keeping watch from the bank with bellies full
of homegrown vegetables

Wharfs undulate with memories of fish
ghosts of kittens and men who never returned

Brings them back to shore in buckets

RUGGED

My bones are brittle
slowly breaking
under the wet
of my rum-soaked skin.
Shades of ash and snow curve
to my chin clinging to,
they say, my heroic face
greeting and saying goodbye
one last time.

They stand in line to kiss the forehead
of the almost dead.
It would not be right—
my hands clasped so firmly
with no movement, no warmth,
a perfectly pressed suit, hair
combed neatly to one side, without
a smoke or grimace.

Once this passage has died
this skin will not be mine,
my bones not so brittle.
I'll be back to my usual self,
too rugged for a coffin.

CREMATION

In the middle of a sickness
I rolled out of bed and fell
through the floors to the sky.

I hovered on my good legs
was swept
from bed
to fire to
water—

swam to sea with
a body made of bone
that disappeared

into the waves leaving
a translucence of myself.

SOAK

We met for black coffee under hickory
making up for strength we could not muster.
People turned their chairs against us. The weight
of our table surpassed the policy of everyday chatter.

They could not look.

Over the next eight months
your mind protested sleep,
argued with food,
resigned itself to a life
without him and

that last private conversation.

You lay there with him wrapped in paper sheets
protecting layers of sickness.

With your hands on the thin skin of his wrist
you felt life pass from him.

Your tears soaked through his bed sheets one last time
and your body drenched itself in his spirit.

WINTER

She thought of her father as the first snow fell.
Fire in the woodstove spat
memories into her basement.

Smells of splintering trees
passing under slate clouds
offered no comfort.

His tools hung on hooks, stiff and muted.
His jacket behind the door whispered dust
onto the tongues of sneakers below.

Outside, snowflakes floated in slow motion.
She squeezed one between
her thumb and index finger.

Looking up, defeated,
she watched them descend
as if everything was falling into place.

CLIMBING

You land from the sky somewhere
between the edge of a shore
and the bottom of a mountain.
Neighbourhoods of snow and ice
threaten to jump
from their heavenly places.

You've grown from boy to man
and you're bigger than you were when you began.
It was a lovely day
for a walk in the woods
against the teasing wind,
the sun not yet ready to sink.

 You've never seen so many mountains.
Their trees trail up the sides
stop in patches and pick up again.
There are circles and seams,
puzzles parted by God or someone else
a little less heavenly.
The sun is warm, and you hike up the hill,
the only being between sky and earth
dressed in nothing but what you need
to get there.

At the top you see the wind across the bay.
You look in my direction
and I wonder if you see me
perched against the curve of a cloud.

SWAN SONG

I thought heaven would give me
everything but I am unlucky
enough to be stuck
with this rattling voice.

If I could sing I would find
everyone that I've ever known, alive
or dead, in graveyards and front lawns.
I would sing of lupines, pink and purple,
partridgeberry jam and bakeapple pie. I
would pick up shells with my voice, carry
them out to sea and back again,
drop them on headstones,
fences and houses—
leaving a trail of soft light colours
and little watery homes.

OPEN

The day I died the clouds turned against the sky
like a furrowing brow, broke
in wrinkles and tears.

It took two hours.
I winked a few times
and was gone.

I took his ring, her baby blanket and a picture
of what could never be.

I could stretch my legs.

I could touch my face.

I could see.

And the sky

opened.

ACKNOWLEDGEMENTS

Thank you to Annamarie Beckel, Dana Blackmore, Mary Dalton, Randall Maggs, Robin McGrath, Stephanie McKenzie, Kerry O'Neill, Marnie Parsons, Chad Pelley, Richard Sawyer, John Steffler, Patrick Warner, and everyone at Breakwater Books.

I'd also like to thank the Writers' Alliance of Newfoundland and Labrador and College of the North Atlantic.

"Isolation" is based on Bronwen Wallace's "The Woman in this Poem" (1987).

Some of the poems in the third section are loosely based on Al Pittman's *Thirty-for-Sixty* (1999).

Thank you to Jenn Anderson, Steph Cashin, Lea Coultas, Meghan Ferguson, Kelly Flynn, Andrea Green, Neala Griffin, Sara Hodder, Grace Humber, Heather Igloliorte, Kirsten McKeown, Jody Patey, Rhonda Leboubon, Trudy-Ann Singh, Michelle Snow, Roxanne Sutton, Kristen Sweetland, Sonya Thorne, Peggy Tremblett, and Michelle Wheeler for your friendship and encouragement.

Thank you to the Cull, Miller, and Fowlow families. Thank you to Mom, Dad, Matt, Jessie, Jordan, and S & T for your unconditional love and support. Thank you to Armondo Fowlow whose dedication to his craft has inspired my life.

FOR DISCUSSION

1. Although these poems can stand independently, there seems to be one central female speaker. Describe her characterization.

2. Many of the poems focus on the body and physical experience. What is the author saying about the body's connection to emotional well-being?

3. What are some of the major themes at work in this collection?

4. Look at the introductory poem in each section. What kind of tone does it set for the rest of the section and how does it relate to the collection as a whole?

5. There are a few pivotal points in this character's life. What do you think are some of these points?

6. Some poems deal with the way we experience landscape and setting. How do you connect to the setting and the physical objects in your life?

7. In the last poem where the speaker describes death from the first person point of view, do you find yourself drawing your own conclusions about the speaker's spiritual beliefs?

8. Are there any particular poems that seem to tell the story of your life or feelings towards a certain subject? How do they relate?

9. Look closely at the poems in the first section. What is the tone? Are there any poems that on first reading seem to have positive tones and on closer examination seem more negative?

10. How does the title poem relate to the collection?

AUTHOR RECOMMENDED SOUNDTRACK

"Ahead by a Century," The Tragically Hip; "Disarm," Smashing Pumpkins; "Arrow of Stones," Pathological Lovers; "Face Up and Sing," Ani Difranco; "We Are All in Love," Jerry Stamp; "Reasons Why," Nickel Creek; "A Case of You," Joni Mitchell; "The River," Bruce Springsteen; "Black Crow Blues," Townes Van Zandt; "Euthanasia," Glyd; "Down Where the Drunkards Roll," Richard Thompson

KERRI CULL is from the small mill town of Corner Brook on the West Coast of Newfoundland. She has been a bartender, bookseller, waitress, administrator, radio show host, columnist, instructor, and is the creator of The Book Fridge. She currently lives in Labrador.

PHOTO: PEGGY TREMBLETT